The GOOD OLD DAYS

45049 The Staffordshire Regiment (The Prince of Wales's Own) and 47374 have picked up some freight from the sidings by York Carriage Works and head off southwards on the York freight avoiding line at 12.47 on 12 August 1981.

Ken Gambles

First published 2021
ISBN 978-1-913390-27-3
© Ken Gambles / Strathwood Publishing 2021
Published by Strathwood, Unit 4 Shuttleworth Road,
Elm Farm Industrial Estate, Bedford, MK41 0EP
Tel 01234 328792 - www.strathwood.co.uk

Right Having just been detached from the stock of its terminating train from Carlisle 47463 moves off from Leeds station at 15.36 on 21 September 1987.

Below. Sand bound for Redfearn's Glassworks (now Ardagh) is seen at Carlton behind 47218. The loco will run round at Cudworth Station before returning to back up on the remains of the ex-Barnsley Court House branch at 07.34 on 15 April 1982.

On the freight avoiding line at Clifton Sidings, York 40193 moves north with a trainload of empty Cobra wagons at 13.54 on 12 August 1981.

FREIGHT TRAFFIC

'THE GOOD OLD DAYS'

A plenitude of pleasing pictures in a panorama of BR power', so might Leonard Sachs have intoned, in his role as MC for 'The Good Old Days', an old-time music hall variety show broadcast from the City Varieties in Leeds and running on BBC from 1953 to 1988.

My own 'good old days' of railway interest began in 1956 at Cudworth near Barnsley on the Midland mainline, and whilst mourning the end of steam I retained sufficient enthusiasm that after qualifications, a job, marriage and children, in 1978 I began to take railway slides before the impending end of the Peaks, 31s, 37s, 40s and Deltics that I had witnessed being introduced in the early 1960s.

Some 3,000 images later and after countless enjoyable hours by the lineside or on railway stations I am now able to offer a varied selection of BR traffic from 1978 to 1990. Of course, most of the motive power is now just history, but I hope that the pictures might give pleasure and bring back happy memories for those who were there at that time.

And so, in the over-hyped alliteration of Leonard Sachs again, 'Please peruse this panoply of polychromatic perspectives from the past in a paroxysm of pleasure' or more simply I hope you enjoy the photos from those 'good old days'.

For the television programmes of the era referenced within the captions, a full list can be found at the end, all photographs have been taken by the author.

Ken Gambles Knaresborough 2021

Opposite: *Blockbusters*. A block working of Tarmac wagons is rolled through the station at Salisbury by 47193, a long way from its Crewe home at 14.36 on 8 August 1983.

Seen on a damp Carlisle afternoon a double-headed trainload of steel coil comes to a halt in the city's station on this occasion the locomotive in view is 86315 at 14.45 on 14 February 1983.

The Good(s) Life. Another locomotive working a long way from its Finsbury Park base this time was 31217, seen busy shunting at Harrogate Goods Yard. At this time there were still regular freight workings from York. The bogie bolster suggests it was steel for Octavius Atkinson at Starbeck. The Bower Street site of the yard is now an ASDA supermarket, this was the lunchtime scene at 13.15 on 26 October 1978.

EARN YOUR STRIPES

Back to work for some after the holidays and 08098 heads a short coal train through a snowy Wakefield Kirkgate at 11.21 on 3 January 1979.

Rattling off the mainline at Hunslet with a mixed freight is a pristine 08423. Assuming the test match against Australia was as good as lost, I went off taking photographs, whilst just a couple of miles away at Headingley Ian Botham and Bob Willis had other ideas while I was here instead at 11.48 on 21 July 1981 during the morning session.

Opposite: It could almost be in a museum as 03107 poses at a litter-free platform 12 of Newcastle Station beneath that magnificent freshly-painted overall roof at 12.13 on 12 April 1980.

Left: *Potter*. Found pottering at Scarborough was 03073 with its regulation match-truck as it waits by Falsgrave signal box ready to couple on to some recently arrived stock and release the train locomotive which was 45066 at 11.05 on 13 August 1983.

Top right: Railmen banter as 08771 pauses briefly in its duties of shunting carriage stock at York at 10.24 on 12 May 1984.

Bottom right: Recently transferred from Ebbw Junction 08579 runs through Wakefield Kirkgate with two wagons and seven hoppers, probably for the glassworks at Castleford on 3 January 1979.

OLD BUFFERS

Opposite: *Birds of a Feather.* A pair of Class 31s involved in track replacement work at Harrogate Station stand in the seldom used sidings to the north of the station as 31247 on the left accompanies an unidentified class member at 13.45 on 23 September 1983.

The end of the line at Weymouth finds 33113 in the station following its right time arrival on the 11.35 ex-London Waterloo. It will form a return working later in the afternoon when seen at 14.18 on 24 July 1981.

The Clayton West branch did well to survive until the 1980s probably due to Park Mill Colliery. E51440 stands in Clayton West Station before its short 30-minute journey back to Huddersfield with the 12.50 departure. Originally the line here was intended to join the Leeds - Barnsley line at Darton. Closure came on 22 January 1983; this view was taken at 12.45 on 4 June 1982.

Opposite: A Departmental single railcar drifts past Cudworth North Junction signal box. The sad remains in the foreground are of the ex-Hull and Barnsley Railway's line which once continued to join the Midland mainline at Cudworth. 09.56 on 15 April 1982.

Based at Thornaby depot on Teesside, 37007 runs light engine south of the site of Cudworth station and passes buffer stops on a little-used siding. Less than a week earlier this Class 37 had been noted as far north as Aberdeen. 09.22 on 14 April 1982.

Opposite: Efforts are being made to clean up oil-bespattered 43052 City of Peterborough in readiness for a return working from Leeds to King's Cross. Presumably the engine in this power car would be shut down, but on its departure, I failed to notice after I took this photograph at 13.50 on 21 September 1987.

Opposite: Clattering northwards past Cudworth North signal box 25060 heads a rake of loaded wagons. It is viewed from the remaining abutments of the impressive ex-Hull & Barnsley Railway's girder bridge which formerly crossed the mainline at this point. 08.58 on 15 April 1982.

Brought to a stand in the through road at Manchester Victoria with its train of oil tanks, 40091 will have a demanding task ahead of it as it tackles the one and a quarter mile long Miles Platting incline, with the gradient varying between 1 in 47 and 1 in 59. This was part of the original route from Manchester to Normanton through the Calder Valley. Bankers were usually available to give assistance on the climb if required. 10.26 on 15 April 1983.

The Generation Game. 56024 brings a loaded merry-go-round coal train past Storrs Mill near Cudworth. The remains of the bridge which can be seen was of an ex-Great Central Railway branch to Houghton and Grimethorpe collieries. It was closed in 1960. Taken at 15.45 on 14 April 1982.

Resplendent in Railfreight sub sector coal livery 56122 heads a Cawoods coal train on the York avoiding line at 13.47 on 30 March 1988.

Opposite: *You've been Framed.* Beneath an overbridge at Rotherham Masboro' a tanker train in charge of 37221 is headed for George Stephenson's original North Midland line to Chesterfield which avoided Sheffield at 10.55 on 19 April 1979.

40046 slogs up the climb from Huddersfield to Standedge Tunnel with a loaded coke train. It is seen on the approach to Marsden from the leading cab of DMU E50284 at 15.48 on 4 June 1982.

ABSTRACTS

Opposite: Diesel and electric traction at Carlisle has grabbed the attention of the spotters. On the left 47143 waits for departure northwards having just taken on coolant. Meanwhile, 85001 has just arrived with a parcels working at 12.26 on 25 October 1980.

Permanent Way staff take a breather to watch 45025 slowing for its York stop with the 09.05 Liverpool to Scarborough service. The girders of Holgate Bridge are in evidence. It was erected by the North Eastern Railway in 1911 and had to be raised in 1989 to allow for the electrification of the East Coast mainline. The site was a favoured position of the local rail enthusiasts. 11.25 on 5 September 1983.

Top: Seen through the broken window of a derelict permanent way hut 33022 approaches Salisbury with the 12.10 Bristol Temple Meads to Portsmouth Harbour service at 13.31 on 8 August 1983.

Bottom: The station canopy and footbridge at Sherborne frame 50049 Defiance getting underway with the 14.15 Exeter St. David's to Waterloo working at 15.39 on 2 August 1983.

Take Hart. A study in black and white, almost like a pen and ink sketch, at Liverpool Lime Street with 86230 at journey's end. I had just arrived from Anfield where I had enjoyed a Sunderland 1-0 win which saved them from relegation. Just over three weeks later on 27 May, Liverpool would go on to win the European Cup in Paris by beating Real Madrid 1-0 with a goal from Alan Kennedy. It was Liverpool's third European Cup win. 17.24 on 2 May 1981.

The day's station pilot at Manchester Victoria was Longsight based 25231 which is seen here shunting at the north-east end of the station at 11.22 on 27 October 1982. This Class 25 had just been transferred from Scotland a few days earlier.

53607 leads the 10.22 Leeds-Harrogate-York service off Knaresborough viaduct and into its Knaresborough stop. The distinctive six-sided signal box of 1875 had a lovely view across the Nidd Gorge and was a busy box, being the commencement of the single line section to Cattal. The original viaduct of 1848 collapsed during building and this replacement dates from 1851. 11.10 on 17 April 1984.

MULTIPLE UNIT DEPARTURES

Opposite: Rail blue days are remembered in this quiet time at Eastbourne as unit 7050 rests in the station at 16.00 on 4 April 1983.

The 13.10 from Westbury to Weymouth gets underway again from Yeovil Pen Mill led by W53820. Here there were links to the Southern mainline at Yeovil Junction and to Yeovil Town with its cross-country branch to Taunton. The route from Weymouth to Bristol Temple Meads is not quick, but travels through some delightful Dorset scenery and the River Avon valley. 13.58 on 9 August 1983.

An interesting arrival at Manchester Victoria where Class 100, M50355 has been paired with Class 105, M50812 on a suburban service at 13.24 on 15 April 1983.

Seen passing Hunslet on the outskirts of Leeds, E51430 hurries the 09.43 Leeds-Barnsley-Sheffield local beneath a surviving signal gantry. This was an area full of sidings and was home to famous locomotive builders of the past such as the Hunslet Engine Co., along with Kitson, Hudswell-Clarke, and Manning Wardle. 09.50 on 22 November 1980.

The on-time 07.57 departure for Crewe leaves Llandudno past the signal box and beneath the semaphore signals. The rear car is M53306 of Chester depot. The journey to Llandudno Junction along the Conwy estuary is one well worth taking. 07.57 on 25 April 1984.

Opposite: *Rising Damp*. There has been a heavy shower at Torre as the 10.10 Paignton to Newton Abbot local calls after its one-mile climb from Torquay. The impressive Grade 2 Listed Great Western signal box of 1921 dominates the scene. Closed in 1988 it is now in private hands. 10.19 on 13 April 1985.

Leading car 51432 is pulling to a halt at leafy Burley-in-Wharfedale with an Ilkley to Leeds working. There was once a junction here which allowed a direct route from Harrogate to Skipton. 10.03 on 31 August 1984.

Opposite: A Manchester-Glossop-Hadfield 3-car set departs Dinting on the 10.43 Hadfield to Manchester Piccadilly, as Class 506 car M59405 brings up the rear at 10.54 on 4 July 1981.

Left: First stop out of Manchester on the electrified route to Bury is Woodlands Road and here M77173 leads the 14.45 from Bury on the last leg of its journey, at 15.05 on 27 October 1982.

Right: This Trans-Pennine unit at York led by E51960 bides the last few minutes before departure with the 15.15 train to Liverpool at 15.10 on 27 October 1978.

No sign of Rod Hull as EMU 410/2 4-BEP 7021 enters Eastbourne on this bright April evening with the 16.40 London Victoria to Ore. 18.04 on 6 April 1983.

Opposite: Appropriately, a Calder Valley unit, rear car 52069 waits to leave Hebden Bridge, with its attractive signage, on a Manchester to York service. A terminated Blackpool train can be seen in the sidings. Buses were in operation owing to work on Holme Tunnel on the Copy Pit line. 12.41 on July 1986.

Catching my eye at the buffer stops at Manchester Piccadilly are on the left 81017 and on the right EMU class 304 unit 022. 14.55 on 4 July 1981.

CROSSING THE LINE

Opposite: Having breasted the 1 in 86 climb from Starbeck the 13.11 York-Harrogate-Leeds local runs past Harrogate North signal box ready for its Harrogate stop. The leading car is E51843 at 13.48 on 28 October 1988.

A dramatic distant sky gives impact to a sunlit Smithy Bridge signal box as 53603 heads over the level crossing and to a stop with a Manchester Victoria working. The lovely signal box was sadly taken out of use and demolished in 2014. 15.34 on 23 July 1986.

Opposite: 50011 Centurion pulls to a halt at Gillingham (Dorset) in charge of the 14.20 Exeter St. David's to Waterloo service at 15.48 on 21 July 1980.

It is a wet afternoon at Poole as almost all eyes are on Unit 421 (with a Class 33 at the rear) as it heads over the crossing by the town's station on its way to Bournemouth and eventually London. 15.25 on 20 August 1985.

Opposite: Looking the other way from page 43 at Smithy Bridge sees 53643 working back across the Pennines with a service to York. The station here, just north of Rochdale, had only recently been re-opened in 1985. 15.21 on 23 July 1986.

With nameplates missing (this side at least) 45014 The Cheshire Regiment crosses Jumble Lane just beyond Barnsley station with a loaded merry-go-round train. There was once a footbridge provided here and the long-closed Barnsley shed (36D) was sited to the right of the locomotive. 13.21 on 14 April 1982.

33115 has made its tentative journey through Weymouth's streets and is entering the yard at Weymouth station prior to joining the mainline. The train is the 15.30 Waterloo boat train and the once familiar pilotmen, bell and flashing light are all in evidence at 15.54 on 27 July 1981.

Traffic waits at Seamer for the 12.25 York to Scarborough to pass on the last stage of its trip to the coast at 13.26 on 13 August 1983.

Crossroads. At Torside Crossing on the Woodhead route, light engines 76027 and 76014 hurry westwards across the Pennines over the A628 under an ominous sky at 16.31 on 29 May 1981.

Opposite: 50036 Victorious is ready to leave Paignton in charge of the 15.45 departure for Exeter St. David's. The Torbay and Dartmouth Steam Railway can be glimpsed on the left. 15.45 on 14 August 1984.

Gardener's World. Daffodils in planters form a pleasant platform feature as set P462 with car 51304 leading runs into Paignton, seven minutes late, with a terminating service from Newton Abbot at 16.27 on 11 April 1985.

Opposite: On the Leeds New Line exit from Leeds, 45123 The Lancashire Fusilier gets into its stride with the 10.33 departure from the city bound for Paignton. The line was built by the LNWR in 1882 and the impressive viaduct skirted Holbeck shed below to the right. 10.40 on 21 July 1981.

Halifax (A 58)
Huddersfield
(A 61)

13′·9″

12′·6″

PASSENGER TRAFFIC

Plenty of custom at Shipley for the 15.52 Ilkley to Bradford Forster Square formed of a Class 144 Pacer Unit. Thirty years later these very basic units were still in service. 16.22 on 25 August 1990.

Opposite: Obeying the rules 33107 gingerly wends its way through the quayside streets of Weymouth at the head of the 15.30 boat train service to London Waterloo at 15.35 on 31 July 1979.

Blake's (4)7. With its rolling stock appropriately in Trans-Pennine livery 47417 rolls to a stop at Platform 15 of York station, heading the 10.17 from Newcastle to Liverpool. The waiting passengers are ready to board their train at 11.51 on 30 March 1988.

With its driver straining for a view 40075 backs on in readiness to couple up to the summer Saturdays only 1M71, the 08.55 York to Llandudno. By December the loco's big ends had seized and it was withdrawn from Gateshead Depot. 08.25 on 22 August 1981.

Opposite: At the head of the 09.45 Manchester Victoria to Blackpool 47537 Sir Gwynedd/County of Gwynedd awaits departure time from the station at 09.39 on 15 April 1983.

In poor weather for a trip to the coast 45043 The King's Own Royal Border Regiment passes Castleford with the seasonal 09.15 from Wakefield Westgate to Scarborough. It would appear its passengers are in for a damp day as they pass by at 09.32 on 22 July 1982.

Approaching Normanton past the site of the now razed Normanton shed (55E) is the four-coach 09.05 Leeds to Poole which will join with a Newcastle portion at Sheffield. On this hazy sunshine morning 47265 is the train engine as it passes at 09.23 on 30 October 1980.

The crowds disgorge for a day at the seaside from the recently arrived 08.33 Wakefield Westgate to Scarborough in a bay platform at the terminus. The flag warns of shattered buffer stops following a recent accident and loco 40085 somehow seems to have acquired a car registration plate. 10.14 on 4 August 1981.

Opposite: *Top Gear*. Viewed from the footbridge by the National Railway Museum in York, cars from now almost four decades ago, throng the carpark as 47530 stands patiently at platform 14 of York station with the 10.05 Liverpool to Newcastle at 12.36 on 5 September 1983.

Wish You Were Here. Passengers will be happy as the sun shines on their arrival at the seaside as 31411 runs into its destination past Falsgrave signal box at Scarborough with the seasonal 07.28 from Huddersfield at 09.52 on 13 August 1983.

A vestige of the once busy Midland mainline route to London, for 1M14 as the 07.58 Leeds to St. Pancras passes Cudworth South Junction signal box in bright sunshine. The return working left St. Pancras at 16.50, but both services were discontinued at the start of the 1982 summer timetable on May 17. Taken at 08.31 on 14 April 1982.

Both driver and a passenger are on the lookout as 40077 is ready to leave Leeds station's platform 6 with a Scarborough train at 09.49 on 1 June 1982.

On the final leg of its journey to the coast at Weymouth, 33109 leaves Dorchester South with the 09.35 from Waterloo due to arrive six minutes after this shot was taken at 12.11 on 27 July 1981.

A traditional view of York station sees 46027 slowing to a halt with the summer Saturdays only 07.26 Luton to Scarborough at 11.54 on 18 June 1983.

Great Rail Journeys of the World. For me, visits to Scotland were rare, but here is a Sprinter unit at Inverkeithing on the 10.40 Dundee to Edinburgh working. It will soon be crossing the magnificent Forth Rail Bridge on its way to Scotland's capital city, taken at 11.40 on 4 April 1989.

47456 thunders through Garforth station north of Leeds with the 09.35 Llandudno to Scarborough, The attractive North Eastern Railway footbridge dates from 1911. Taken at 13.12 on 24 June 1983.

Runaround. Its stock having been released 40028 (formerly named *Samaria*) backs on to what was the rear of its train as a railman waits to couple up. Alongside Gateshead depot's 47413 waits on a Glasgow extra at 11.40 on 13 August 1983.

45117 squeals as it swings round the sharp curve at Miles Platting station at the head of the 11.00 Scarborough to Liverpool at 13.30 on 27 October 1982.

Duties finished for the time being 25199 and 25145, both of Longsight wait outside the shed at Reddish before separating and then entering the depot at 12.40 on 4 July 1981.

TWO OF A KIND

Brush Strokes. 31205 and 31113 keep each other company in the afternoon sunshine outside York shed at 17.23 on 11 June 1982.

Opposite: The double-headed trainload of steel coil (as seen on page 5) was seen first from the road bridge to the north of Carlisle Station a double-headed trainload of steel coil is easing to a halt behind 86035 and 86315, both of Willesden Depot at 14.30 on 14 February 1983.

The Professionals. The crew of 47079 G.J. Churchward of Cardiff Canton wait to be relieved from the navy contingent special 1Z24, at rest in Leeds station. The nameplate is a shortened version of the original George Jackson Churchward. 16.01 on 16 April 1980.

The local radio station 'Pennine' neatly captions first generation units E51502 (in the foreground) and E51504 at rest in Huddersfield station at 12.44 on 18 February 1980.

Opposite: 20066 and 20131 drift under the girders of Holgate Bridge at York with a rake of mineral wagon empties. As was often the case a group of young spotters is in attendance. 12.57 on 23 August 1982.

A track maintenance train is seen at Goose Hill Junction, Normanton in charge are 25060 and 25196, taking the Wakefield route, probably bound for Healey Mills Yard at 13.10 on 1 June 1982.

This ballast train passes Dringhouses, York with an interesting English Electric duo of 40047 and 37006 in charge at 09.36 on 21 August 1982.

With power applied ready to tackle the steep Miles Platting incline 37002 and 37201 surge through Manchester Victoria with a tanker train probably from Stanlow at 10.40 on 15 April 1983.

DELTIC DEMISE

The 'A' Team. Deltics at Newcastle on top link duties, on the right 55011 The Royal Northumberland Fusiliers has just arrived with the 09.00 King's Cross to Edinburgh. Owing to the collapse of Penmanshiel Tunnel the train would terminate at Berwick. Alongside, 55022 Royal Scots Grey waits to take over for the remainder of the journey at 13.00 on 28 April 1979.

Another sighting of 55022 Royal Scots Grey this time running into York station with the 09.50 Edinburgh to Plymouth. It will be replaced here by 47500 Great Western to continue the onward journey to the South-West. 13.36 on 22 October 1979.

Opposite: DMU E50155 and a luggage trolley frame 55011 The Royal Northumberland Fusiliers as it waits to take over a train to the North at York station at 13.30 on 11 April 1980.

The 07.22 Plymouth to Edinburgh has been brought into York by a Class 47 which is now being replaced by 55019 Royal Highland Fusilier, seen here through a coach window, backing on at 14.35 on 14 August 1980.

Grandstand. Its 12.54 on 3 May 1980 as 55005 The Prince of Wales's Own Regiment of Yorkshire moves off from Doncaster past its admirers with the 12.15 York to King's Cross. It was Rugby League Cup Final Day featuring local rivals Hull F.C. and Hull Kingston Rovers.

Opposite: York's platform 3 finds 55009 Alycidon at rest with engines off to reduce noise and fume pollution after its arrival from London with the 15.10 from King's Cross. 15.15 on 21 June 1980.

For some reason 55014 The Duke of Wellington's Regiment has been detached from the 08.47 Bridlington to King's Cross at York and is being replaced by 55015 Tulyar, seen backing on with a host of interested parties in attendance at 10.55 on 13 June 1981.

This time it is the turn of 55004 Queen's Own Highlander to stand at rest in platform 3 of York station following its arrival with the 16.05 from King's Cross at 19.10 on 30 May 1980.

Opposite: A lovely portrait of 55005 The Prince of Wales's Own Regiment of Yorkshire moving off shed at York ready to collect its stock from the carriage sidings for the 10.45 departure for King's Cross. The locomotive was named at York on 30 September 1963. 10.18 on 4 October 1980.

Opposite: Light and silhouettes at Newcastle where 55008 The Green Howards awaits the right of way with the 09.50 Edinburgh to Plymouth. As usual there is plenty of platform interest in the Deltic at 11.55 on 12 April 1980.

Happy Days. The nameplate rubbers get to work on 55004 Queen's Own Highlander following its arrival on the 16.05 from King's Cross. (see also page 88). 19.10 on 30 May 1980.

With the single line token accepted, 55009 Alycidon accelerates away from a snowbound Knaresborough with 1G06 'The Deltic Executive' following its photo stop in Harrogate. 12.25 29 December 1981.

Opposite: *Blankety-Blank.* A snow flurry greets leading car 51556 at Cattal as it comes off the single line section from Knaresborough with an on-time 13.22 Leeds-Harrogate-York train. 14.20 on 24 January 1984.

SNOW WORRIES

Bob Bryant, one of Knaresborough's signalmen, always made me welcome and here, seen from the box, he collects the single line token from E51815 on the 11.22 York-Harrogate-Leeds local at 11.48 on 29 December 1981.

Opposite: *Panorama*. The Nidd Gorge at Knaresborough makes a beautiful sight in the snow. The 12.22 from Leeds crosses the viaduct at 13.20 on 24 January 1984.

TV Programmes referred to in Ceefax style.
Cover: The Good Old Days BBC 1953 - 1983
p.4 Blockbusters ITV 1983 - 1993
p.6 The Good Life BBC 1975 - 1978
p.10 Potter BBC 1979 - 1983
p.12 Birds of a Feather BBC 1989 - 1998
p.20 The Generation Game BBC 1971 - 2002
p.22 You've Been Framed ITV 1990 - the present
p.27 Take Hart BBC 1977 - 1983
p.30 Blue Remembered Hills 'Play for Today' by Dennis Potter BBC 1979
p.35 Rising Damp Yorkshire TV 1974 - 1978
p.39 Emu's Broadcasting Company ITV 1975 - 1980
p.50 Crossroads ITV 1964 - 1988
p.52 Gardener's World BBC 1968 - the present
p.55 Blake's 7 BBC 1978 - 1983
p.62 Top Gear BBC 1977 - the present
p.63 Wish You Were Here ITV 1974 - 2003
p.68 Great Railway Journeys of the World BBC 1980
p.70 Runaround ITV 1975 - 1981
p.73 Brush Strokes BBC 1986 - 1991
p.75 The Professionals London Weekend TV 1977 - 1983
p.81 The 'A' Team BBC 1983 – 1987
p.85 Grandstand BBC 1958 - 2007
p.86 Happy Days ABC 1974 - 1984
p.93 Blankety-Blank BBC 1979 - 1990
p.95 Panorama BBC 1953 - the present
p.96 Ceefax BBC 1974 - 2012

A Sheffield to Leeds local is silhouetted at
Normanton on a cold winter's day at 14.45
on 3 January 1979.